2024 Barndominium Floor Plans and Designs

A Collection of Stylish and Functional Designs Just For You

Rosita O. White

Contents

Introduction

Welcome to the realm of Bardominiums, where the perfect blend of elegance, efficiency, and modern design harmonizes with rustic charm. Within the pages of this book, we extend a warm invitation to embark on a captivating journey through a meticulously curated collection of Bardominium floor plans. Each plan serves as a testament to the seamless fusion of comfort, functionality, and aesthetic appeal.

Bardominiums have experienced a surge in popularity in recent years, captivating the hearts of homeowners in search of a distinctive and versatile living space. Originally inspired by the fusion of barn and condominium, these unique dwellings have evolved into a distinct architectural style that effortlessly combines the best of both worlds. With their open-concept layouts, soaring ceilings, and a tasteful balance of rustic and refined finishes, Bardominiums offer a refreshing departure from conventional home designs.

Within the confines of this book, you will uncover an inspiring array of floor plans expertly crafted to suit various lifestyles and preferences. Whether your vision entails a cozy retreat nestled amidst rolling countryside or a spacious urban oasis in the heart of the city, our collection showcases a diverse range of designs tailored to cater to your individual needs.

From charming one-bedroom retreats to expansive layouts perfect for families, each floor plan has been meticulously designed to optimize space utilization and facilitate a seamless flow between living areas. Every detail has been carefully considered, ensuring that each crevice and corner exudes the essence of Bardominium living. Picture sun-drenched great rooms, gourmet kitchens adorned with reclaimed wood accents, and luxurious master suites that beckon relaxation and rejuvenation.

Beyond their captivating aesthetics, Bardominiums are renowned for their adaptability. As you peruse the pages of this book, you will encounter floor plans that effortlessly accommodate various functions, whether it's a home office, an entertainment space, or a private guest suite. The versatility of these designs empowers homeowners to unleash their creativity and personalize their living spaces to suit their ever-evolving needs.

We wholeheartedly invite you to immerse yourself in the enchanting world of Bardominiums and embark on a journey of inspiration and discovery. Allow the pages of this book to serve as your guide as you explore the boundless possibilities that lie within these captivating homes. Each floor plan is a testament to the extraordinary harmony between rustic charm and contemporary living, a testament to the enduring allure of the Bardominium lifestyle.

One-Story Barndominium-Style House Plan with 2-Story Interior

Welcome to this meticulously crafted single-story barndominium-style house plan, where the timeless charm of a barn seamlessly merges with the modern comforts of a contemporary home. The exterior exudes elegance with its classic board and batten facade, featuring clean lines and expansive windows that flood the interior with natural light while establishing a harmonious connection with the surrounding landscape. Adding to its allure, a covered patio and a delightful pergola create an inviting outdoor sanctuary, blurring the boundaries between indoor and outdoor living.

As you approach the residence, you'll be greeted by a welcoming covered patio that leads to a spacious foyer. Stepping through the front door, you'll discover the heart of the home—a stunning open-concept living area that seamlessly integrates the kitchen, dining, and living spaces.

Inside, lofty ceilings amplify the sense of spaciousness, while a striking fireplace serves as both a source of warmth and a captivating focal point. Floor-to-ceiling windows and double French doors gracefully open to the patio, offering breathtaking views of the outdoors and facilitating a seamless indoor-outdoor living experience.

The patio, an extension of the living space, has been thoughtfully furnished with comfortable outdoor seating, providing an idyllic vantage point to appreciate the natural surroundings. Adjacent to the patio, the attached pergola offers additional shade and creates the perfect ambiance for alfresco dining or moments of relaxation.

Immerse yourself in the charm and comfort of this thoughtfully designed barndominium-style house plan. Its exceptional blend of rustic elegance and contemporary living ensures a truly remarkable living experience, both indoors and outdoors.

Floor Plan

Main Level

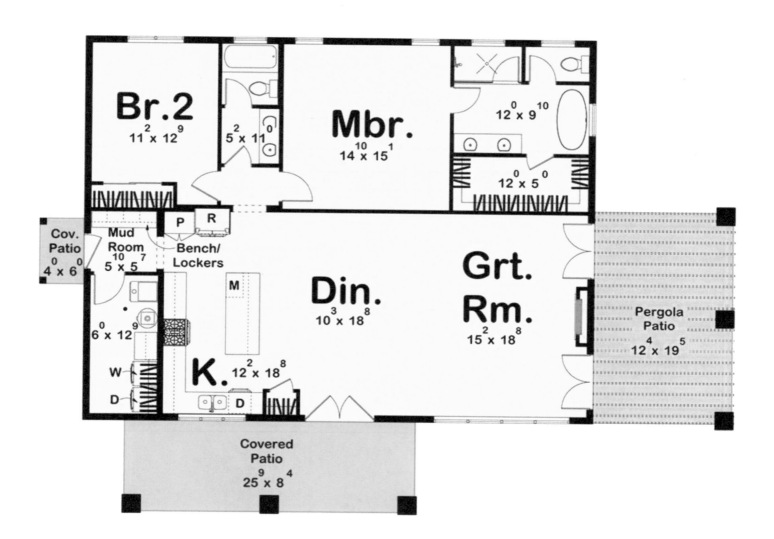

Plan details

Square Footage Breakdown
Total Heated Area:1,575 sq. ft.
1st Floor:1,575 sq. ft.
Porch, Combined:238 sq. ft.
Beds/Baths
Bedrooms:2
Full Bathrooms:2
Foundation Type
Standard Foundations: Slab
Optional Foundations: Walkout, Crawl, Basement
Exterior Walls
Standard Type(s):2x6
Dimensions
Width:61' 4"
Depth:43' 4"
Max Ridge Height:18' 11"
Ceiling Heights
Floor / Height: First Floor / 9' 0"
Roof Details
Primary Pitch:3 on 12

2-Bed Barndominium with Cathedral Ceilings

Experience the ultimate rural living with this exquisite 2-bedroom Barndominium boasting an impressive 3,187 square feet of luxurious living space. Adding a touch of charm, a weathervane gracefully sits atop the cupola, serving as the perfect finishing touch.

As you approach the home, your attention will be drawn to the barn doors positioned at the center of the front elevation, beckoning you to step inside and discover the heart of this remarkable residence. The interior seamlessly blends with an open utility room, offering convenience and functionality.

Prepare to be captivated by the enormous family room, destined to become the centerpiece of countless holiday gatherings. Its grandeur is accentuated by a soaring cathedral ceiling adorned with exposed beams, lending a rustic and inviting aesthetic.

Indulge in the warmth and ambiance of the double-sided fireplace, accessible from both the family room and the covered porch, creating an ideal setting for relaxation and outdoor enjoyment. Additionally, a bonus room provides a versatile space that can easily adapt to your evolving needs and preferences.

The bedrooms, thoughtfully positioned on the main level, frame the heart of the home. Each bedroom boasts a full bath and a spacious walk-in closet, ensuring comfort and privacy. Upstairs, a generous loft awaits, providing endless possibilities for use as a playroom, home office, or even a personal gym.

Embrace the unparalleled allure of this 2-bedroom Barndominium with cathedral ceilings. Its meticulously designed floor plan and versatile spaces offer an exceptional living experience, perfectly tailored to meet the demands of a modern lifestyle.

REAR ELEVATION

Floor Plan

Main Level

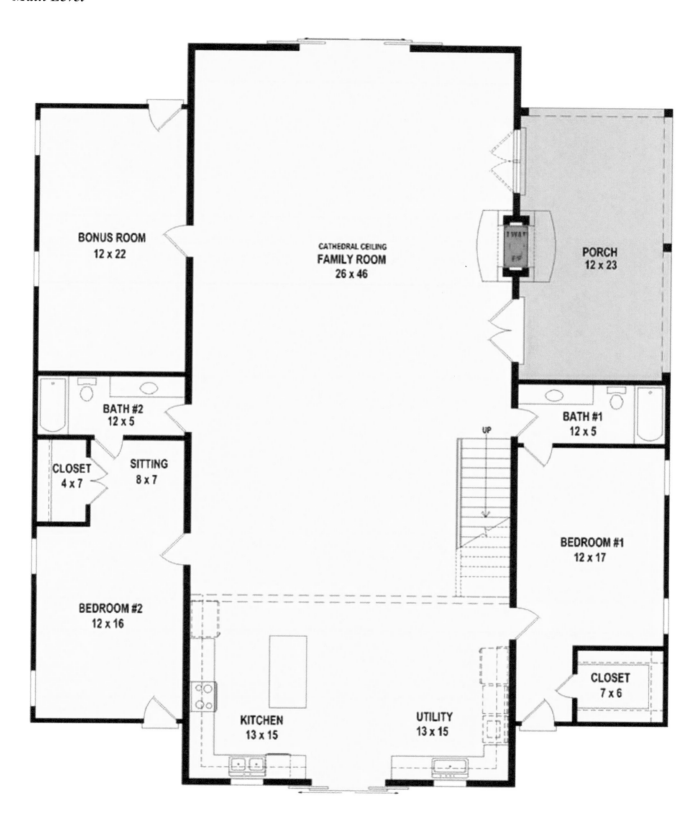

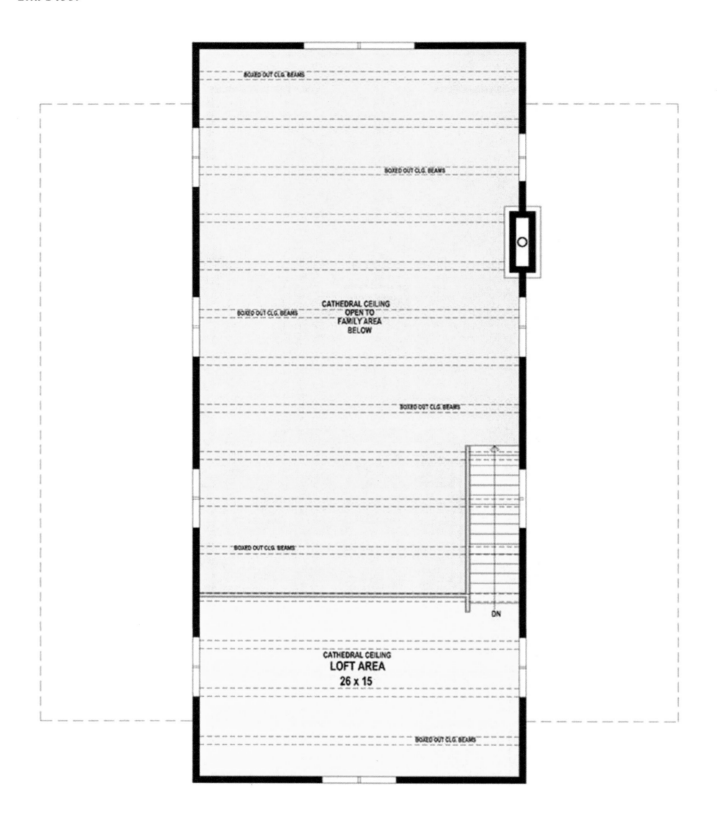

Plan details

Square Footage Breakdown
Total Heated Area:3,187 sq. ft.
1st Floor:2,692 sq. ft.
2nd Floor:495 sq. ft.
Screened Porch:283 sq. ft.
Beds/Baths
Bedrooms:2
Full Bathrooms:2
Foundation Type
Standard Foundations: Slab
Exterior Walls
Standard Type(s):2x4
Optional Type(s):2x6
Dimensions
Width:51' 10"
Depth:62' 4"
Max Ridge Height:24' 3"
Ceiling Heights
Floor / Height: First Floor / 10' 0"
Roof Details
Primary Pitch:4 on 12

New American Garage Apartment Plan with Barndominium Styling

Indulge in the perfect fusion of New American style and Barndominium charm with this extraordinary two-story carriage house plan. The exterior is a sight to behold, boasting captivating wood accents and garage doors adorned with board and batten siding, resulting in a visually stunning facade that will leave a lasting impression.

Prepare to be amazed as you explore the interior of this exceptional garage apartment. The main level features a spacious three-car garage, providing ample room to accommodate your vehicles and storage needs. Moving to the upper level, you'll discover a thoughtfully designed apartment that offers a versatile living space above.

Upon stepping inside, you'll be greeted by an inviting living room and kitchen area arranged in an open layout, perfectly suited for modern living and entertaining. The kitchen is a dream come true for culinary enthusiasts, showcasing an expansive island that serves as a focal point, providing both functionality and style. Additionally, a convenient walk-in pantry ensures that you have abundant storage space to keep your kitchen organized and well-stocked.

Experience the best of both worlds with this remarkable 2-story carriage house plan. Its harmonious blend of New American style and Barndominium charm delivers a truly exceptional living experience. From the striking exterior to the thoughtfully designed interior, this home showcases the perfect balance of style, functionality, and comfort.

Floor Plan

Main Level

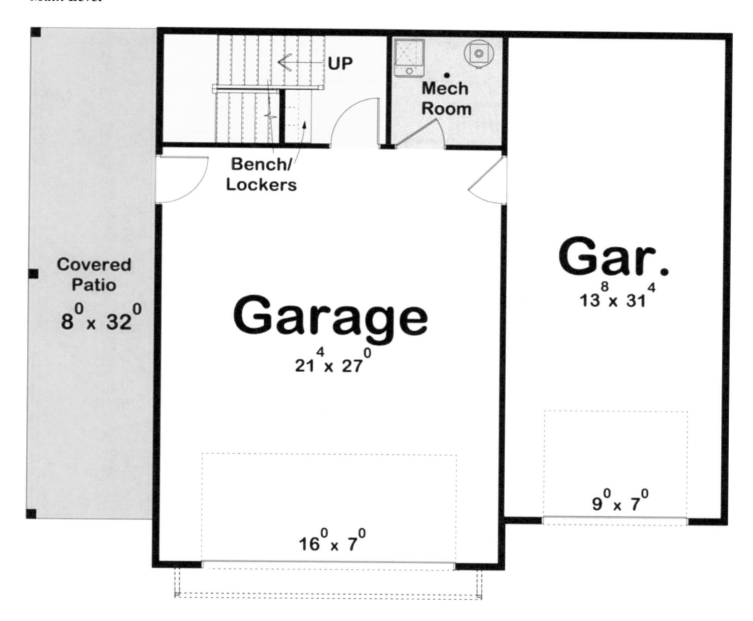

21

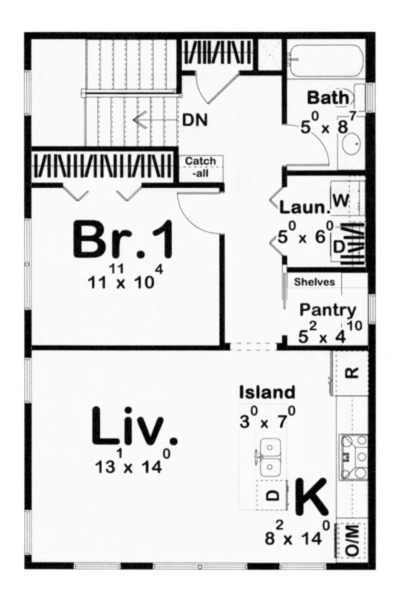

Plan details

Square Footage Breakdown
Total Heated Area:767 sq. ft.
2nd Floor:767 sq. ft.
Covered Patio:256 sq. ft.

Beds/Baths
Bedrooms:1
Full Bathrooms:1

Foundation Type
Standard Foundations: Slab

Exterior Walls
Standard Type(s):2x4
Optional Type(s):2x6

Dimensions
Width:44' 0"
Depth:35' 0"
Max Ridge Height:28' 0"

Garage
Type: Attached
Area:1144 sq. ft.
Count:3 cars
Entry Location: Front

Ceiling Heights
Floor / Height: First Floor / 9' 0"Second Floor / 9' 0"

Roof Details
Primary Pitch:8 on 12
Secondary Pitch:3 on 12

RV-Friendly Barndo-style House Plan with Carport and Home Office

Introducing a remarkable barndo-style house plan, affectionately known as a "shouse" due to its unique blend of a shop and a house. This exceptional design features four spacious garage bays, each equipped with its own 10' by 10' garage door, providing ample space for parking and storage.

On the side, a generously-sized 16' by 16' overhead door offers convenient clearance for your RV or boat, ensuring easy access for your outdoor adventures. To further enhance the functionality of this home, a sprawling 60'-wide carport extends across the entire width of the property, offering shelter and protection for all your vehicles.

Step inside to discover a well-planned interior layout. Two bedrooms are thoughtfully clustered together, creating a private space for rest and relaxation. Additionally, a third room is dedicated as a home office, providing a tranquil environment for work or study. With the bedrooms and office conveniently grouped, the remaining portion of the home is dedicated to an open living space shared by the living room and kitchen/dining area.

The heart of this open concept area features an inviting island, providing casual seating and serving as a central gathering spot for family and friends. Adding character and warmth is a wood stove, which not only adds aesthetic appeal but also provides cozy heat during colder months. This open space seamlessly blends functionality and style, creating a harmonious environment for everyday living.

Embrace the allure of this barndo-style house plan, where the perfect combination of practicality and charm converges. With its spacious garage bays, versatile living spaces, and thoughtful design elements, this home is truly a haven for those seeking a distinctive and functional dwelling.

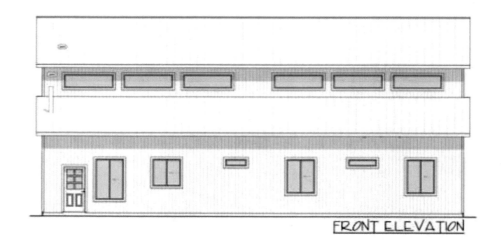

FRONT ELEVATION

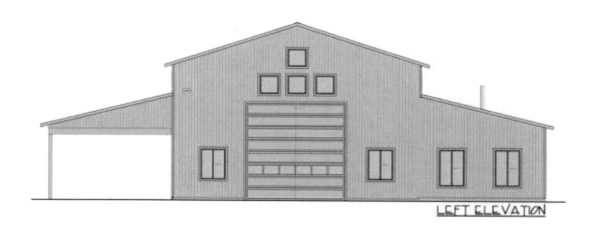

LEFT ELEVATION

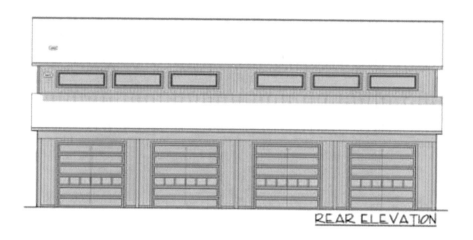

REAR ELEVATION

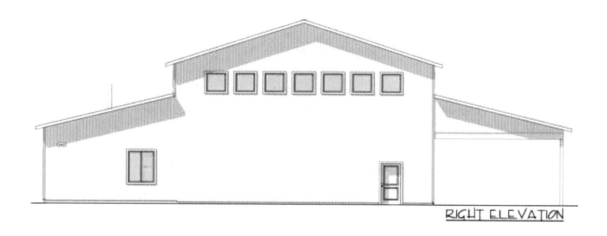

RIGHT ELEVATION

Floor Plan
Main Level

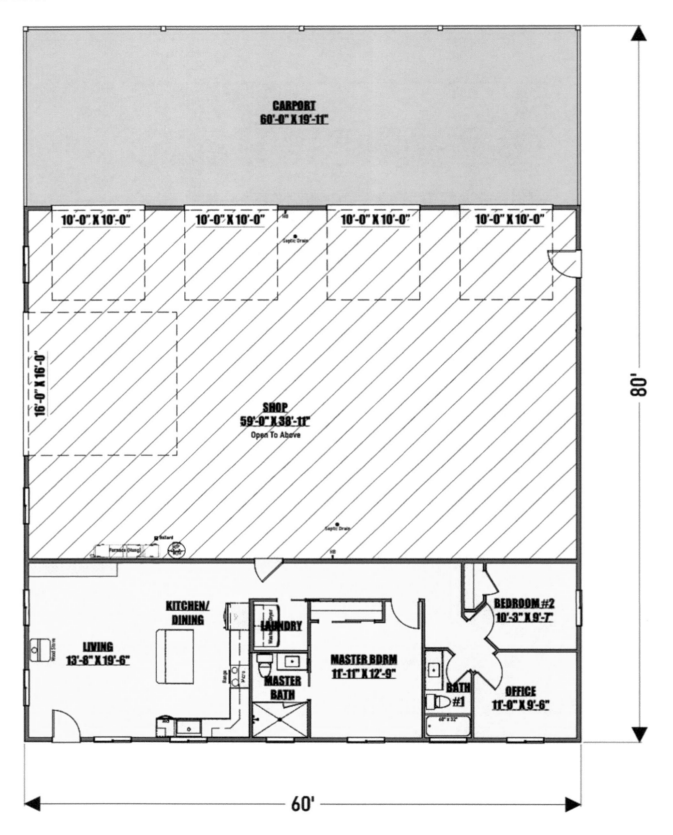

CARPORT
60'-0" X 19'-11"

10'-0" X 10'-0"   10'-0" X 10'-0"   10'-0" X 10'-0"   10'-0" X 10'-0"

16'-0" X 16'-0"

SHOP
59'-0" X 38'-11"
Open To Above

Septic Drain

Septic Drain

80'

60'

KITCHEN/
DINING

LAUNDRY

BEDROOM #2
10'-3" X 9'-7"

LIVING
13'-8" X 19'-6"

MASTER BDRM
11'-11" X 12'-9"

MASTER
BATH

BATH
#1

OFFICE
11'-0" X 9'-6"

Plan details

Square Footage Breakdown

Total Heated Area:1,230 sq. ft.	
1st Floor:1,230 sq. ft.	
Carport:1,200 sq. ft.	
Carport:1,200 sq. ft.	

Beds/Baths

Bedrooms:2	
Full Bathrooms:2	

Foundation Type

Standard Foundations: Slab

Exterior Walls

Standard Type(s):2x6

Dimensions

Width:60' 0"	
Depth:80' 0"	
Max Ridge Height:29' 0"	

Garage

Type: RV Garage, Attached	
Area:2370 sq. ft.	
Count:4, 5, 6, 7, or 8 cars	
Entry Location: Rear, Side	

Ceiling Heights

Floor / Height: First Floor / 11' 0"

Room Details	Ceiling Type	Width	Depth	Height
Workshop	Vaulted	59' 0"	38' 11"	21' 9" to 26' 9"

Roof Details

Primary Pitch:4 on 12	
Secondary Pitch:3 on 12	
Framing Type: Truss	

Barndominium-Style House Plan with Home Office and Oversized RV Garage

Welcome to this remarkable barndominium-style house plan, distinguished by its stick-framed construction that showcases the timeless charm of board and batten siding, wood accents, and wood garage doors. The exterior is further enhanced by a welcoming large wrap-around porch, inviting guests into the home with its warm and inviting ambiance.

Step through the front French doors and you'll find yourself in the entryway, with the great room lying just ahead. The great room boasts an impressive 2-story ceiling and features a captivating fireplace flanked by built-in benches with convenient drawers. This space is perfect for gathering and entertaining. Adjacent to the great room, you'll discover the well-appointed kitchen, complete with a spacious island that doubles as a snack bar, a walk-in pantry, and ample counter space for all your culinary needs. Tucked away behind the kitchen is a fantastic home office, providing a quiet and productive space for work or study.

Towards the rear of the home, a generously-sized formal dining room awaits. This elegant space boasts its own set of French doors that lead to the rear portion of the wrap-around covered porch, creating an ideal setting for outdoor dining or relaxation.

Conveniently located on the main floor, the master suite offers a tranquil retreat. The master bathroom is designed for luxury and functionality, featuring his and her vanities, a wet room with a soaking tub, a large walk-in closet, and direct access to the laundry room, ensuring convenience and ease of use.

Upstairs, you'll find three additional bedrooms, each boasting its own walk-in closet, providing ample storage space for personal belongings. Overlooking the great room below, a wonderful loft area adds an element of charm and versatility to the home's design.

Returning to the main level, the home's massive oversized 3-car garage offers ample space for vehicles and storage. Its notable features include an RV door for easy access and 14' ceilings, accommodating larger vehicles or providing additional storage opportunities.

Embrace the allure of this barndominium-style house plan, where thoughtful design elements and luxurious features converge to create a haven of comfort and style.

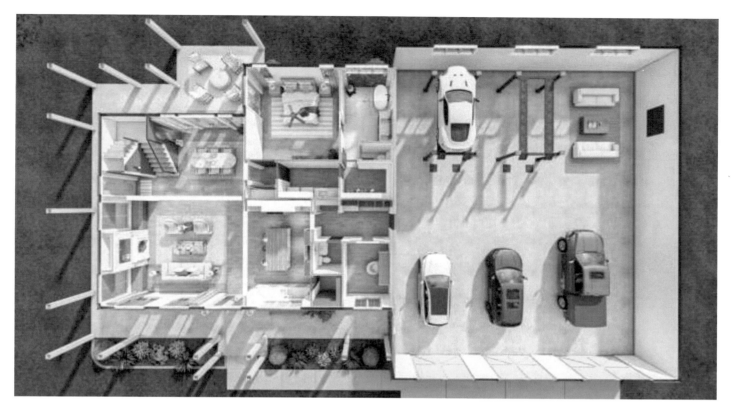

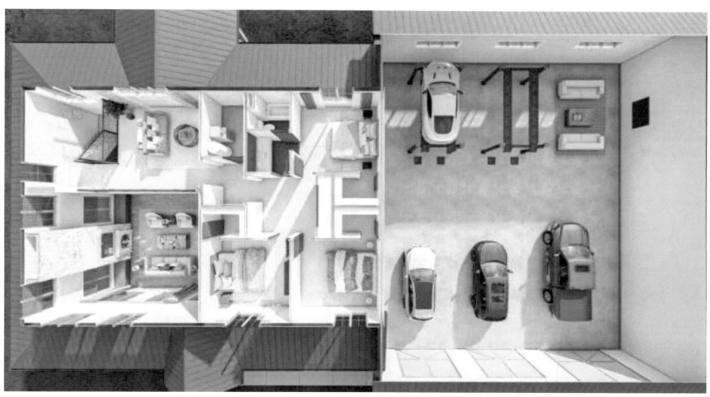

Floor Plan

Main Level

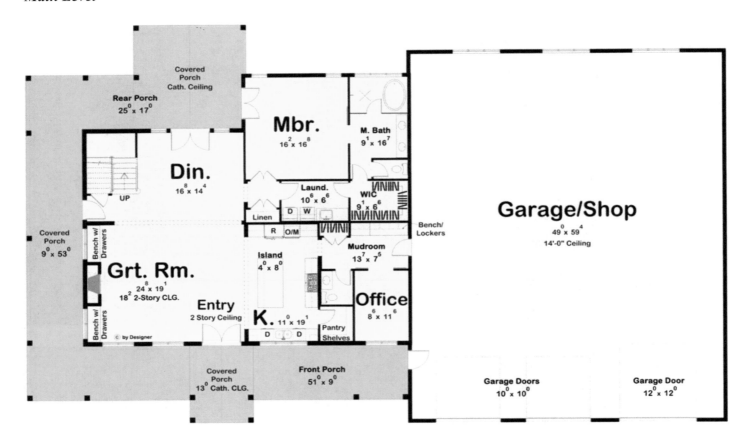

2nd Floor

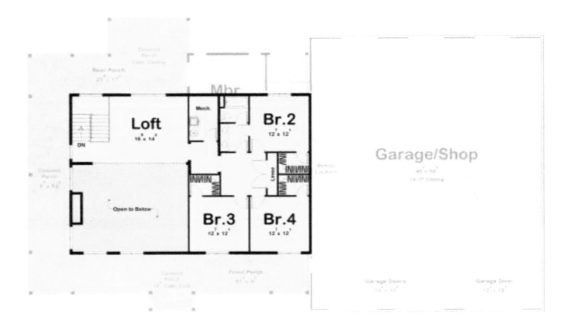

Plan details

Square Footage Breakdown
Total Heated Area:3,293 sq. ft.
1st Floor:2,043 sq. ft.
2nd Floor:1,250 sq. ft.
Porch, Rear:425 sq. ft.
Porch, Front:459 sq. ft.

Beds/Baths
Bedrooms:4
Full Bathrooms:2
Half Bathrooms:1

Foundation Type
Standard Foundations: Slab
Optional Foundations: Walkout, Crawl, Basement

Exterior Walls
Standard Type(s):2x6

Dimensions
Width:110' 0"
Depth:64' 8"
Max Ridge Height:30' 0"

Garage
Type: RV Garage, Attached
Area:2998 sq. ft.
Count:3 cars
Entry Location: Front

Ceiling Heights
Floor / Height: First Floor / 9' 0"Second Floor / 8' 0"

Roof Details
Primary Pitch:6 on 12
Secondary Pitch:3 on 12
Framing Type: Stick And Truss

4-Bed Barndominium with Open Living Space and Storage Mezzanine

Experience the perfect blend of simplicity and convenience with this remarkable Barndominium plan, setting it apart as a standout design.

Attached to the right side of the home, you'll find an oversized garage that offers ample space for your vehicles and storage needs. This garage features a storage mezzanine measuring 36'2" wide by 8'4" deep, providing additional storage space to keep your belongings organized and easily accessible.

As you step onto the property, the inviting wraparound porch welcomes you into the open living room and island kitchen. The living room is adorned with a fireplace, adding a touch of warmth and ambiance to the living space. This open layout creates an inviting atmosphere, perfect for entertaining and creating lasting memories.

The master bedroom is thoughtfully positioned towards the rear of the main level, ensuring privacy and tranquility. It also enjoys convenient access to the laundry room, adding a touch of convenience to daily routines.

Upstairs, a generous loft area leads to three bedrooms, providing comfortable and private spaces for family members or guests. These bedrooms share a full bathroom equipped with a linen closet and a double-sink vanity, ensuring that everyone's needs are met.

The exterior finish of this exceptional Barndominium plan is specified with corrugated metal siding, enhancing its aesthetic appeal and durability.

Embrace the simplicity, convenience, and charm of this remarkable Barndominium plan, where thoughtful design and functional spaces come together to create an extraordinary living experience.

48

Floor Plan

Main Level

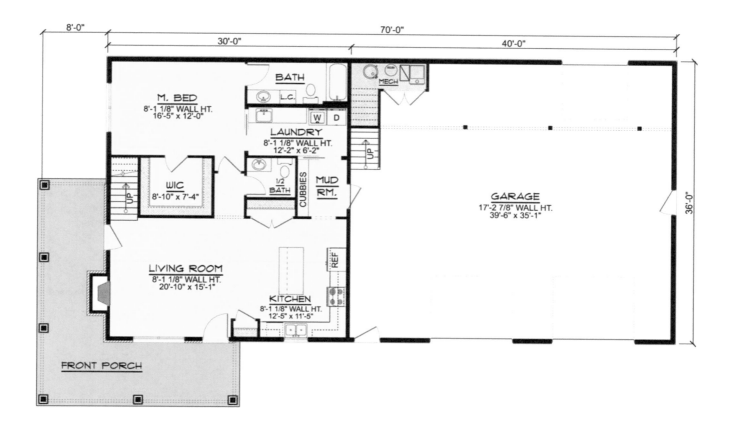

2nd Floor

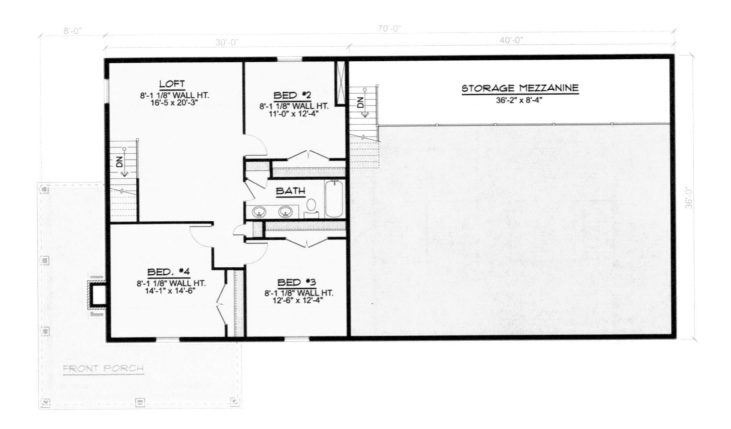

LOFT
8'-1 1/8" WALL HT.
16'-5 x 20'-3"

BED #2
8'-1 1/8" WALL HT.
11'-0" x 12'-4"

STORAGE MEZZANINE
36'-2" x 8'-4"

DN

BATH

BED. #4
8'-1 1/8" WALL HT.
14'-1" x 14'-6"

BED #3
8'-1 1/8" WALL HT.
12'-6" x 12'-4"

FRONT PORCH

8'-0"   30'-0"   70'-0"   40'-0"   36'-0"

50

Plan details

Square Footage Breakdown
Total Heated Area:2,152 sq. ft.
1st Floor:1,080 sq. ft.
2nd Floor:1,072 sq. ft.
Storage:362 sq. ft.
Porch, Combined:371 sq. ft.
Beds/Baths
Bedrooms:4
Full Bathrooms:2
Half Bathrooms:1
Foundation Type
Standard Foundations: Slab
Optional Foundations: Walkout, Crawl, Basement
Exterior Walls
Standard Type(s):2x6
Dimensions
Width:78' 0"
Depth:44' 0"
Max Ridge Height:23' 0"
Garage
Type: Attached
Area:1440 sq. ft.
Count:3 cars
Ceiling Heights
Floor / Height: First Floor / 8' 0"Second Floor / 8' 0"
Roof Details
Primary Pitch:4 on 12
Framing Type: Truss

Barndominium-Style House Plan with 2-Beds and an Oversized Garage

Explore the perfect living space with this delightful barndo-style house plan, providing a generous 1,587 heated square feet. It is an ideal size for a small family, a couple, or anyone seeking additional space without the burden of overwhelming maintenance.

As you approach the front of the home, you'll be welcomed by a covered patio, offering a cozy outdoor space to relax and enjoy the surroundings. Upon entering, you'll be captivated by the cathedral ceilings that create an open and airy ambiance, enhancing the overall sense of spaciousness.

Step inside to reveal a spacious area that seamlessly blends the kitchen, great room, and dining room. The open floor plan enhances the perception of space, making the area feel even larger than its actual size. This design fosters a warm and inviting atmosphere, perfect for entertaining and spending quality time with loved ones.

Continuing throughout the plan, you'll discover a convenient mudroom, along with two well-appointed bedrooms. The master bedroom boasts a walk-in closet with direct access to the laundry room, ensuring practicality and efficiency in your daily routines. Both bathrooms feature double vanities, providing ample space to accommodate guests while avoiding any sense of crowding.

The backyard is equally inviting, featuring a covered porch where you can unwind and appreciate the views after a long day, creating a serene retreat right at home.

This plan is perfect for those who desire the distinctive barndominium style while remaining within a budget. It offers a practical and functional layout, combined with stylish design elements, allowing you to create a comfortable and inviting home without straining your finances. Enjoy the best of both worlds with this charming barndo-style house plan.

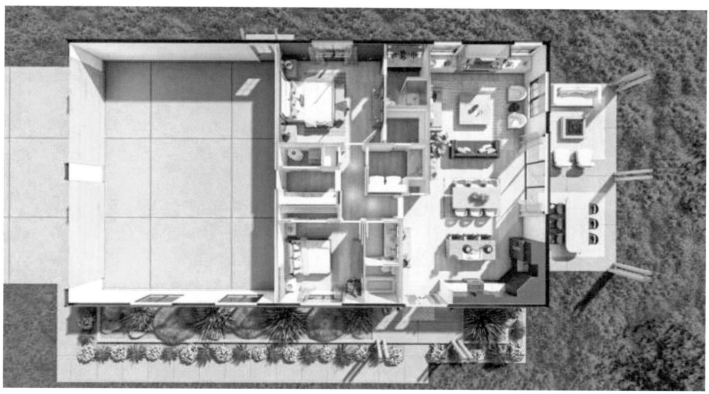

Floor Plan

Main Level

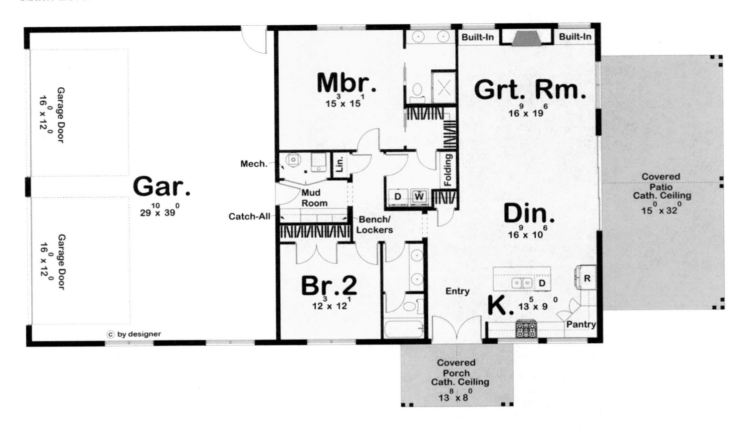

Plan details

Square Footage Breakdown
Total Heated Area:1,587 sq. ft.
1st Floor:1,587 sq. ft.
Porch, Combined:589 sq. ft.
Beds/Baths
Bedrooms:2
Full Bathrooms:2
Foundation Type
Standard Foundations: Slab
Optional Foundations: Walkout, Crawl, Basement
Exterior Walls
Standard Type(s):2x6
Dimensions
Width:85' 0"
Depth:48' 0"
Max Ridge Height:24' 7"
Garage
Type: Attached
Area:1213 sq. ft.
Count:4 cars
Entry Location: Side
Ceiling Heights
Floor / Height: First Floor / 14' 0"
Roof Details
Primary Pitch:6 on 12
Framing Type: Truss

Barndominium-Style House Plan with Side and Rear Garage Access

Experience the perfect blend of rustic charm and modern comfort with this versatile barndominium-style carriage house plan. This two-story structure offers a spacious and functional layout, catering to both your living and storage needs.

Upon entering the home, you'll be welcomed by a bench and locker drop zone, providing a convenient space to organize your belongings. A well-placed bathroom offers comfort and convenience, while a concrete safe room provides peace of mind during severe weather or emergency situations. The main floor features a large garage, offering ample room to accommodate your vehicles, recreational equipment, or even serve as a workshop for your projects.

Ascending the staircase to the upper level, you'll find yourself in the heart of the home—a captivating and open great room that seamlessly combines the living, kitchen, and dining areas into a single expansive space. This open concept design encourages interaction and easy entertaining, making it the perfect gathering place for family and friends.

The kitchen is thoughtfully designed with modern appliances, plentiful counter space, and a functional island, ensuring that every culinary endeavor is a delight.

Three bedrooms are strategically placed in a split layout, offering private sanctuaries for rest and relaxation. The master bedroom boasts its own luxurious bathroom, complete with a walk-in shower, soaking tub, elegant fixtures, and a spacious walk-in closet, providing a tranquil retreat within the home. The other two bedrooms are situated on the opposite side of the house and share a well-appointed hall bathroom, ensuring privacy and convenience for all occupants.

Embrace the harmonious blend of rustic charm and modern comforts with this exceptional barndominium-style carriage house plan. Its versatile design offers a functional living space while providing ample storage solutions, creating a truly remarkable home for your lifestyle.

Floor Plan

Main Level

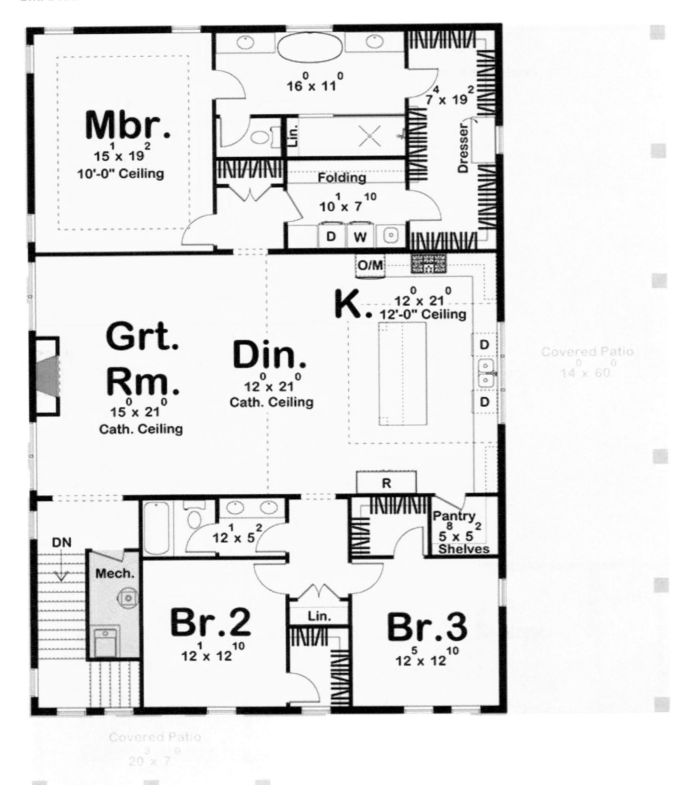

Plan details

Square Footage Breakdown

Total Heated Area:2,569 sq. ft.

1st Floor:282 sq. ft.

2nd Floor:2,287 sq. ft.

Porch, Combined:981 sq. ft.

Beds/Baths

Bedrooms:3

Full Bathrooms:3

Foundation Type

Standard Foundations: Slab

Exterior Walls

Standard Type(s):2x6

Dimensions

Width:54' 0"

Depth:67' 0"

Max Ridge Height:32' 8"

Garage

Type: Attached

Area:2054 sq. ft.

Count:4 cars

Entry Location: Rear, Side, Front

Ceiling Heights

Floor / Height: First Floor / 12' 0"Second Floor / 9' 0"

Roof Details

Primary Pitch:6 on 12

Secondary Pitch:3 on 12

2000 Square Foot Barndominium-Style House Plan with 5-Car Garage

Experience the perfect blend of functionality and style with this exceptional 2-bedroom barndominium-style home. Built with 2x6 framing, this residence offers 2,016 square feet of heated living space, complemented by a remarkable 2,446 square foot 5-car side-load garage. The garage is a true marvel, featuring two 18' by 10' overhead doors on either side of a center bay that is RV-friendly and equipped with 12' by 14' overhead doors.

As you step inside, you'll be greeted by a spacious living room adorned with a fireplace and cathedral ceiling. This inviting space seamlessly connects to the island kitchen and the dining room, creating an open and cohesive layout. Sliding doors lead to a vaulted screened porch at the back, providing a serene and relaxing outdoor retreat.

The bedrooms are thoughtfully clustered together on the right side of the home, ensuring a sense of privacy and convenience. The master suite, positioned at the back, is a true oasis. It boasts a pair of French doors that open to a covered porch, allowing you to enjoy the fresh air and outdoor views.

Embrace the perfect combination of functionality and elegance with this remarkable 2-bedroom barndominium-style residence. Its well-designed layout, spacious garage, and stylish features make it an exceptional choice for those seeking comfort, versatility, and a touch of luxury in their living space.

Floor Plan

Main Level

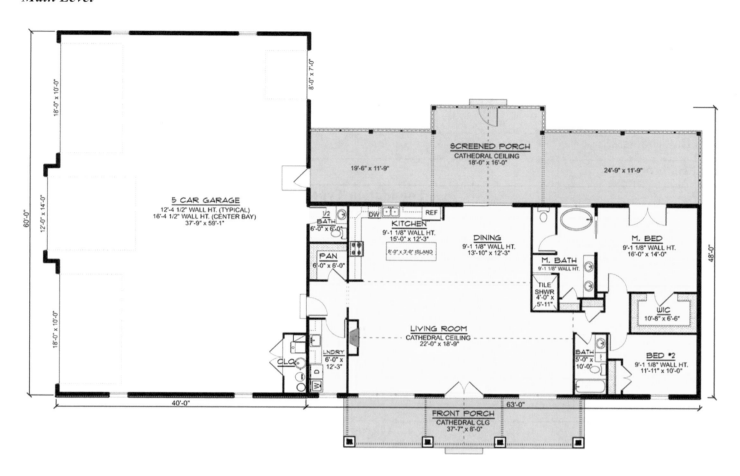

5 CAR GARAGE
12'-4 1/2" WALL HT. (TYPICAL)
16'-4 1/2" WALL HT. (CENTER BAY)
37'-9" x 59'-1"

18'-0" x 10'-0"

12'-0" x 14'-0"

18'-0" x 10'-0"

60'-0"

40'-0"

8'-0" x 7'-0"

SCREENED PORCH
CATHEDRAL CEILING
18'-0" x 16'-0"

19'-6" x 11'-9"

24'-9" x 11'-9"

48'-0"

1/2 BATH
6'-0" x 6'-0"

DW

REF

KITCHEN
9'-1 1/8" WALL HT.
15'-0" x 12'-3"

8'-9" x 3'-0" ISLAND

DINING
9'-1 1/8" WALL HT.
13'-10" x 12'-3"

M. BED
9'-1 1/8" WALL HT.
16'-0" x 14'-0"

PAN
6'-0" x 6'-0"

M. BATH
9'-1 1/8" WALL HT.

TILE SHWR
4'-0" x 5'-11"

WIC
10'-8" x 6'-6"

LIVING ROOM
CATHEDRAL CEILING
22'-0" x 18'-9"

LNDRY
6'-0" x 12'-3"

CLO

W D

BATH
5'-0" x 10'-0"

BED #2
9'-1 1/8" WALL HT.
11'-11" x 10'-0"

63'-0"

FRONT PORCH
CATHEDRAL CLG
37'-7" x 8'-0"

79

Plan details

Square Footage Breakdown
Total Heated Area:2,016 sq. ft.
1st Floor:2,016 sq. ft.
Porch, Combined:1,130 sq. ft.
Beds/Baths
Bedrooms:2
Full Bathrooms:2
Half Bathrooms:1
Foundation Type
Standard Foundations: Crawl
Optional Foundations: Slab, Walkout, Basement
Exterior Walls
Standard Type(s):2x6
Dimensions
Width:105' 0"
Depth:68' 0"
Max Ridge Height:21' 10"
Garage
Type: RV Garage, Attached
Area:2446 sq. ft.
Count:5 cars
Entry Location: Side
Ceiling Heights
Floor / Height: First Floor / 9' 0"
Roof Details
Primary Pitch:8 on 12
Secondary Pitch:6 on 12

3500 Square Foot Barndominium-Style House with Home Office and Oversized Side Entry Garage and Shop

Experience the ultimate blend of functionality and style with this remarkable 3-bedroom Barndominium-style house plan, designed with stick framing. Enjoy the convenience of merging your work and living spaces seamlessly. Nestled on a side-sloping lot, this home capitalizes on its surroundings with a wraparound porch and deck, offering stunning views.

The side-entry garage/shop is a standout feature, boasting a total area of 2,585 square feet. It encompasses three overhead doors, including a generously sized 12' by 14' door in the center bay. This garage/shop provides ample space for parking vehicles, storing equipment, and pursuing your hobbies.

Inside the home, minimal walls separate the kitchen, dining area, and living room, creating the sought-after open-concept layout. This design fosters a sense of spaciousness and promotes effortless flow between the different areas. The island kitchen is both functional and stylish, featuring abundant storage space and a convenient walk-in pantry nearby.

A quiet den is situated just off the entryway, offering a secluded space for relaxation or work. Additionally, an office is located at the back of the garage, providing a dedicated area for professional tasks or personal projects.

81

The master suite, complete with a five-fixture bath and a walk-in closet, is the sole bedroom on the main floor. Upstairs, two more bedrooms await, each equipped with its own walk-in closet. These bedrooms share a well-appointed bathroom. A loft area overlooking the living room below adds a touch of charm and versatility to the upper level.

The exterior finish of this home is specified with corrugated metal siding, lending a unique and contemporary aesthetic.

Embrace the perfect combination of convenience, style, and functionality with this exceptional 3-bedroom Barndominium-style house plan. Its well-designed layout, spacious garage/shop, and beautiful features make it an ideal choice for those seeking a modern and versatile living space.

Floor Plan

Main Level

2nd Floor

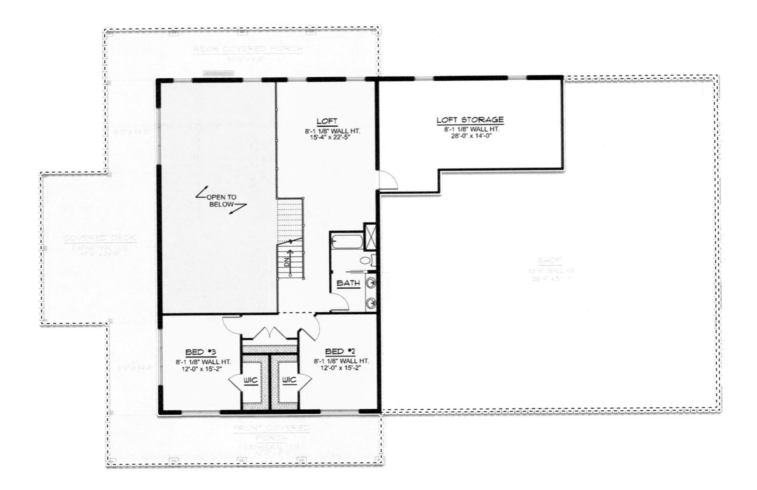

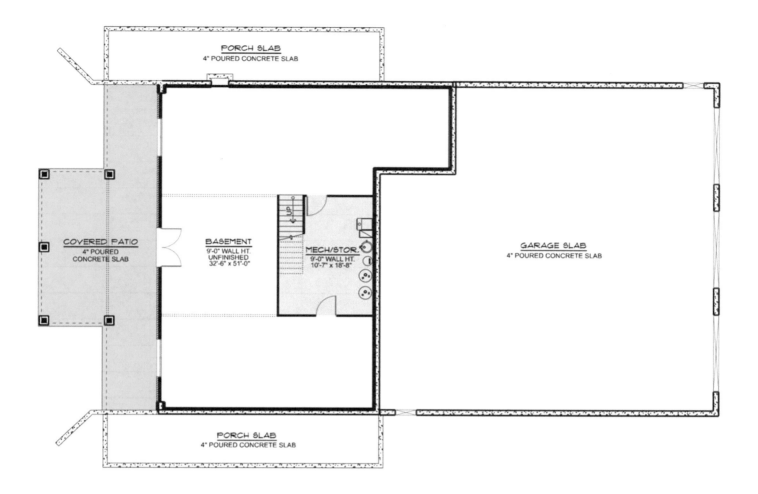

PORCH SLAB
4" POURED CONCRETE SLAB

COVERED PATIO
4" POURED
CONCRETE SLAB

BASEMENT
9'-0" WALL HT.
UNFINISHED
32'-6" x 51'-0"

UP

MECH/STOR.
9'-0" WALL HT.
10'-7" x 18'-8"

GARAGE SLAB
4" POURED CONCRETE SLAB

PORCH SLAB
4" POURED CONCRETE SLAB

Plan details

Square Footage Breakdown
Total Heated Area:3,502 sq. ft.
1st Floor:1,973 sq. ft.
2nd Floor:1,529 sq. ft.
Covered Patio:691 sq. ft.
Deck:685 sq. ft.
Porch, Combined:672 sq. ft.
Basement Unfinished:1,973 sq. ft.
Beds/Baths
Bedrooms:3
Full Bathrooms:2
Half Bathrooms:2
Foundation Type
Standard Foundations: Walkout
Optional Foundations: Slab, Crawl, Basement
Exterior Walls
Standard Type(s):2x6
Dimensions
Width:104' 0"
Depth:69' 0"
Max Ridge Height:28' 9"
Garage
Type: RV Garage, Attached
Area:2585 sq. ft.
Count:3 cars
Entry Location: Front
Ceiling Heights
Floor / Height: Lower Level / 9' 0"First Floor / 9' 0"Second Floor / 8' 0"
Roof Details
Primary Pitch:6 on 12
Secondary Pitch:7 on 12
Framing Type: Truss

Barndominium Style House Plan with Cathedral Ceilings in the House and Garage

Indulge in the beauty of this exquisite Barndominium Style House Plan, offering an impressive 3,258 square feet of heated living space and 424 square feet of outdoor space. The exterior seamlessly blends the simplicity of barn aesthetics with modern design elements, showcasing a captivating combination of wood and metal siding, expansive windows, and a welcoming front porch. Step inside and discover a home that effortlessly merges the timeless charm of a classic barn with the comforts of modern living, creating a truly inviting and unique living space.

Upon entering, you'll be greeted by a grand cathedral ceiling that stretches throughout the open-concept kitchen, dining, and great room area. This expansive and light-filled space serves as the heart of the home, offering a perfect gathering place for family and friends. The soaring ceiling not only enhances the sense of openness but also adds a touch of rustic allure with exposed trusses and an abundance of natural light pouring in from the large windows and doors.

On the opposite side of the house, you'll find an oversized 3-car garage, featuring a spacious overhead door thoughtfully designed to accommodate boats, campers, or any other recreational vehicles. Inside the garage, the cathedral ceiling adds a sense of spaciousness, allowing for ample storage or workshop needs. This ensures that the garage serves a dual purpose of utility and style, catering to all your practical requirements. Embrace the perfect union of classic charm and contemporary living with this exceptional Barndominium Style House Plan. Its thoughtfully designed layout, inviting outdoor spaces, and a blend of rustic and modern elements make it an ideal choice for those seeking a truly remarkable and comfortable home.

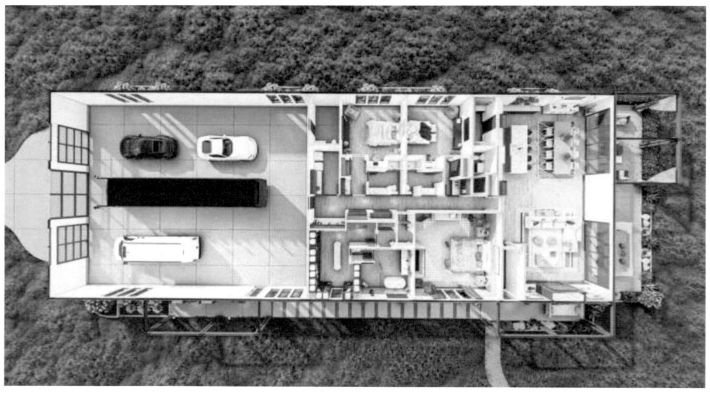

Floor Plan

Main Level

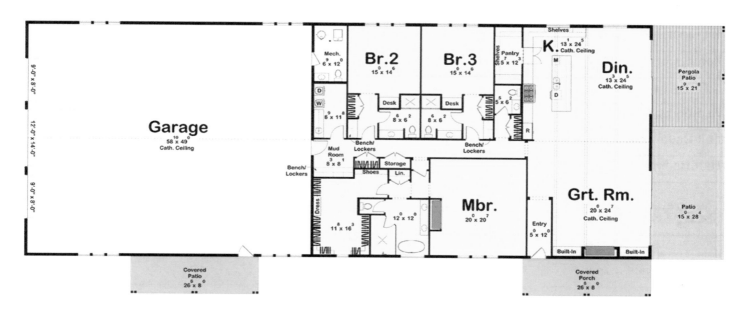

Plan details

Square Footage Breakdown
Total Heated Area:3,258 sq. ft.
1st Floor:3,258 sq. ft.
Porch, Combined:424 sq. ft.

Beds/Baths
Bedrooms:3
Full Bathrooms:3
Half Bathrooms:2

Foundation Type
Standard Foundations: Slab

Exterior Walls
Standard Type(s):2x6

Dimensions
Width:145' 0"
Depth:58' 0"
Max Ridge Height:25' 1"

Garage
Type: RV Garage, Attached
Area:2972 sq. ft.
Count:3 cars
Entry Location: Side

Ceiling Heights
Floor / Height: First Floor / 12' 0"

Room Details	Ceiling Type
Garage	Cathedral
Dining Room	Cathedral
Great Room	Cathedral

Roof Details
Primary Pitch:6 on 12
Framing Type: Truss

Contemporary Barndominium House Plan with Side-Entry Garage

Experience the perfect blend of contemporary design and functionality with this spacious and modern barndominium-style house plan. Designed to be wide and shallow, this residence offers ample parking space for four cars parked tandem-style, providing 1,002 square feet of dedicated parking area. The cars can easily access the parking area through two 9' by 8' overhead doors positioned on the right side of the house.

Inside, the main floor features a versatile flex room, offering endless possibilities for customization based on your needs. Additionally, the combined living space upstairs provides a generous 1,878 square feet of heated living area.

Upstairs, the space is flooded with natural light, thanks to the expansive front windows. The ceiling height gradually increases from 7' at the back to an impressive 12' at the front, creating a sense of openness and grandeur.

The left half of the upstairs encompasses an open floor plan, seamlessly connecting the kitchen, dining area, and living room. This layout is perfect for entertaining guests and fostering a cohesive atmosphere. The kitchen boasts a large island, providing both functional workspace and a gathering spot for socializing.

On the right side of the upstairs, two bedrooms share a well-appointed bathroom. The primary bedroom (Bed 1) enjoys the added luxury of a spacious walk-in closet, providing ample storage space for personal belongings.

Embrace the contemporary charm and practicality of this remarkable barndominium-style house plan. Its well-designed layout, dedicated parking area, and stylish features make it an ideal choice for those seeking a modern and versatile living space.

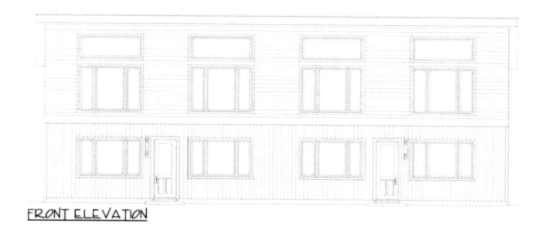

FRONT ELEVATION

LEFT ELEVATION

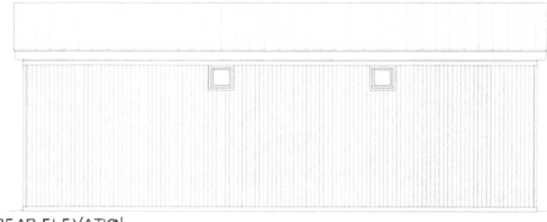

REAR ELEVATION

RIGHT ELEVATION

Floor Plan

Main Level

2nd Floor

Plan details

Square Footage Breakdown
Total Heated Area:1,878 sq. ft.
1st Floor:438 sq. ft.
2nd Floor:1,440 sq. ft.
Beds/Baths
Bedrooms:2
Full Bathrooms:1
Foundation Type
Standard Foundations: Slab
Optional Foundations: Basement, Walkout
Exterior Walls
Standard Type(s):2x6
Dimensions
Width:60' 0"
Depth:24' 0"
Max Ridge Height:24' 9"
Garage
Type: Attached
Area:1002 sq. ft.
Entry Location: Side
Ceiling Heights
Floor / Height: First Floor / 10' 0"Second Floor / 12' 0"
Roof Details
Primary Pitch:2.5 on 12
Framing Type:Stick

Barndo-Style RV Garage with 4320 Square Feet of Parking Space

Experience the ultimate in RV garage house plans with this exceptional barndo-style design. Boasting four garage doors and three bays, this residence offers an impressive 4,320 square feet of parking space for all your vehicles. The middle two doors open up to create a double-wide bay, providing ample room for larger vehicles or equipment.

Inside the house, stairs are conveniently located both indoors and outdoors, offering easy access to a vast loft-like space above. This expansive area provides endless possibilities, allowing you to customize it to suit your needs and preferences.

Whether you envision it as a versatile storage space, a recreational area, or a workshop, the giant loft-like space offers the flexibility to bring your creative ideas to life.

Embrace the convenience and versatility of this extraordinary barndo-style RV garage house plan. Its spacious parking area and expansive loft space make it an ideal choice for those seeking ample storage for vehicles and a customizable area to suit their specific lifestyle.

FRONT ELEVATION

REAR ELEVATION

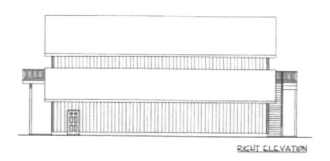

RIGHT ELEVATION

Floor Plan

Main Level

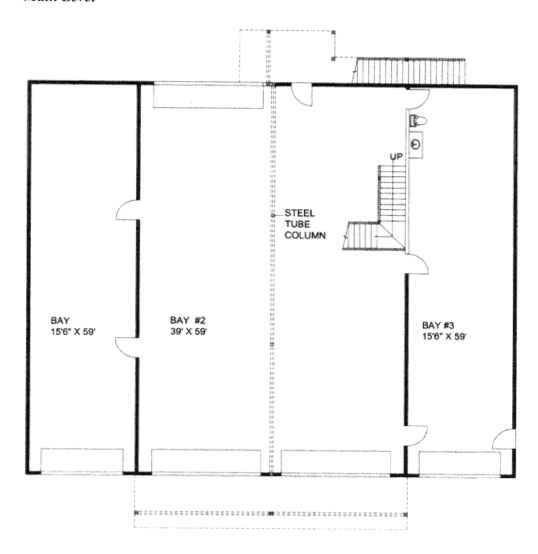

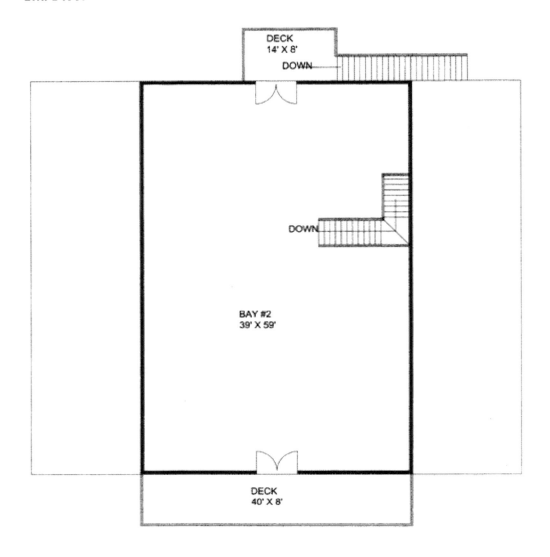

DECK
14' X 8'

DOWN

DOWN

BAY #2
39' X 59'

DECK
40' X 8'

Plan details

Square Footage Breakdown
Total Heated Area:0 sq. ft.
Attic:2,400 sq. ft.
Beds/Baths
Bedrooms:
Full Bathrooms:
Foundation Type
Standard Foundations: Slab
Exterior Walls
Standard Type(s):2x6
Dimensions
Width:72' 0"
Depth:60' 0"
Max Ridge Height:34' 2"
Garage
Type: Detached, RV Garage
Area:4320 sq. ft.
Count:3 cars
Entry Location: Front
Ceiling Heights
Floor / Height: First Floor / 14' 8"
Roof Details
Primary Pitch:6 on 12
Secondary Pitch: N on N

Barndominium with Side-Entry Garage and 2-Story Great Room

Discover the perfect blend of affordability and low-maintenance living with this exceptional Barndominium design. This thoughtfully crafted home offers a harmonious combination of living and garage spaces, providing both comfort and functionality.

As you step inside, you'll be greeted by a welcoming 7'-deep porch that leads you into a spacious great room with tall ceilings. This open-concept area seamlessly flows into the island kitchen, creating a central hub for everyday living and entertaining. Adjacent to the dining room, a covered porch awaits, offering an ideal space for outdoor grilling or alfresco dining.

Convenience meets relaxation on the main level, where the master bedroom is conveniently located. This private retreat features a 4-fixture bathroom, a walk-in closet, and direct access to a 7' by 8'5" safe room, providing peace of mind and security.

Upstairs, a generous loft area offers additional gathering space, perfect for a secondary living area or a media room. Three almost identical bedrooms are situated side by side, and across the hall, you'll find a compartmentalized bath, providing privacy and convenience for family members or guests.

Enter from the 1,559 square foot garage and discover a well-designed mudroom, framed by the laundry room and a powder bath. This functional space serves as a transition area between the garage and the main living area, offering storage and organization for everyday essentials.

The exterior finish of this home is specified with corrugated metal siding, adding a unique and contemporary touch to its overall aesthetic.

Embrace the charm and practicality of this remarkable Barndominium design, offering a well-balanced combination of living and garage spaces. Its thoughtful layout, convenient features, and stylish finishes make it an ideal choice for those seeking an affordable and low-maintenance home.

Floor Plan

Main Level

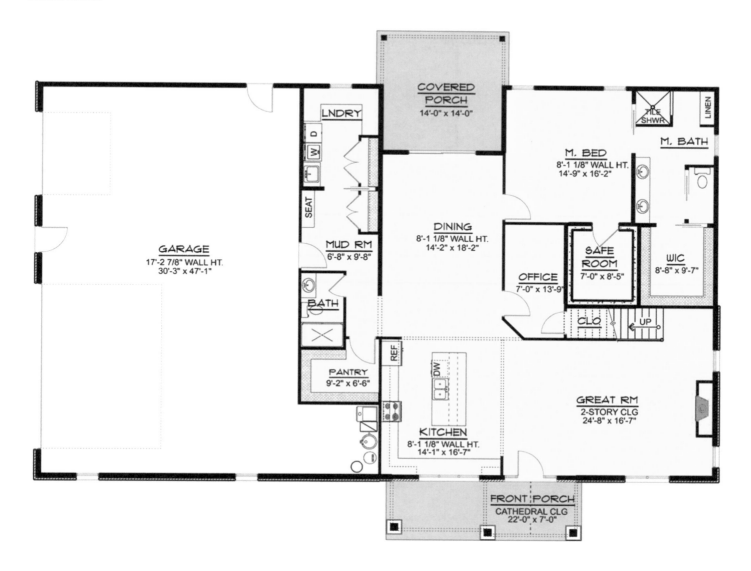

GARAGE
17'-2 7/8" WALL HT.
30'-3" x 47'-1"

LNDRY

W D

SEAT

MUD RM
6'-8" x 9'-8"

BATH

PANTRY
9'-2" x 6'-6"

REF

DW

KITCHEN
8'-1 1/8" WALL HT.
14'-1" x 16'-7"

COVERED PORCH
14'-0" x 14'-0"

DINING
8'-1 1/8" WALL HT.
14'-2" x 18'-2"

OFFICE
7'-0" x 13'-9"

SAFE ROOM
7'-0" x 8'-5"

CLO

UP

M. BED
8'-1 1/8" WALL HT.
14'-9" x 16'-2"

TILE SHWR

LINEN

M. BATH

WIC
8'-8" x 9'-7"

GREAT RM
2-STORY CLG
24'-8" x 16'-7"

FRONT PORCH
CATHEDRAL CLG
22'-0" x 7'-0"

115

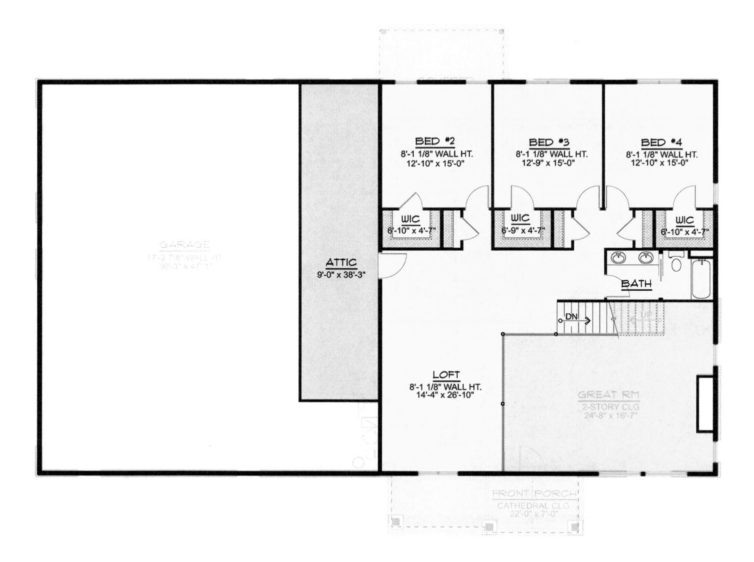

Plan details

Square Footage Breakdown
Total Heated Area:3,569 sq. ft.
1st Floor:2,165 sq. ft.
2nd Floor:1,404 sq. ft.
Attic:364 sq. ft.
Porch, Combined:383 sq. ft.
Beds/Baths
Bedrooms:4
Full Bathrooms:3
Foundation Type
Standard Foundations: Slab
Optional Foundations: Walkout, Crawl, Basement
Exterior Walls
Standard Type(s):2x6
Dimensions
Width:80' 0"
Depth:61' 0"
Max Ridge Height:25' 9"
Garage
Type: RV Garage, Attached
Area:1559 sq. ft.
Count:3 cars
Entry Location: Side
Ceiling Heights
Floor / Height: First Floor / 8' 0"Second Floor / 8' 0"
Roof Details
Primary Pitch:4 on 12
Secondary Pitch:8 on 12

4590 Sq Ft Barndominium Style House Plan with Apartment Behind 1090 Sq Ft Garage

Experience the spaciousness and versatility of this remarkable 6-bedroom barndominium-style house plan. With 4,590 square feet of heated living space and a 1,090 square foot 2-car garage, this home offers ample room for comfortable living. The garage also features a guest apartment behind it, perfect for in-law accommodations, multi-generational living, or rental purposes. A full wraparound porch adds to the charm and functionality of this exceptional residence. Please note that the apartment is included in the total living area.

Upon entering, you'll be welcomed into an open entryway that flows seamlessly into the great room. The great room boasts a cozy fireplace and elegant French doors that lead to the back porch, creating a perfect indoor-outdoor connection.

The kitchen is a culinary delight, featuring an island with seating for up to four people, a convenient walk-in pantry, and an open layout that connects it to both the dining room and the great room. This design promotes effortless entertaining and a seamless flow between spaces.

Privacy and functionality are maximized with a split bedroom layout. The master suite occupies the entire right side of the home and includes an office that can be accessed through a pocket door from the bedroom. This setup allows for a private and convenient workspace. Bedroom 2 is located across the home and has direct access to Bath 2, providing comfort and convenience for residents or guests.

Upstairs, a spacious loft overlooks the great room below and serves as a versatile gathering space. Flanking the loft are two pairs of matching bedrooms, each measuring 14' by 12', and connected by Jack and Jill baths. This arrangement offers flexibility and comfort for family members or visitors.

This house plan was designed with a Pre-Engineered Metal Building (PEMB) in mind, which is a commonly used structure for building barndominiums. PEMBs are engineered, fabricated, and shipped to any location in the world, allowing for efficient installation compared to traditionally framed homes. They also expedite the project timeline and facilitate convenient interior build-outs, as they do not require extensive roof load support.

For added durability and insulation, this metal house plan is available with 2x6 exterior framing. Simply select this option from the menu to enhance the structural integrity and energy efficiency of the home.

Embrace the spaciousness, versatility, and convenience of this exceptional barndominium-style house plan. With its well-designed layout and practical features, it offers a comfortable and stylish living space for families of all sizes.

121

Floor Plan

Main Level

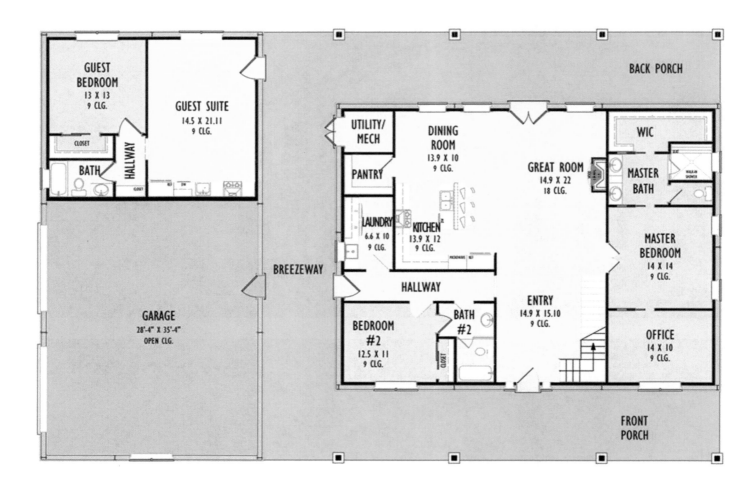

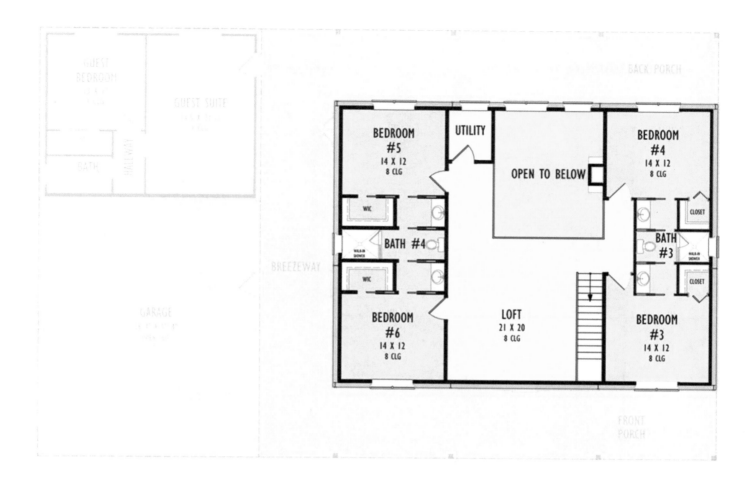

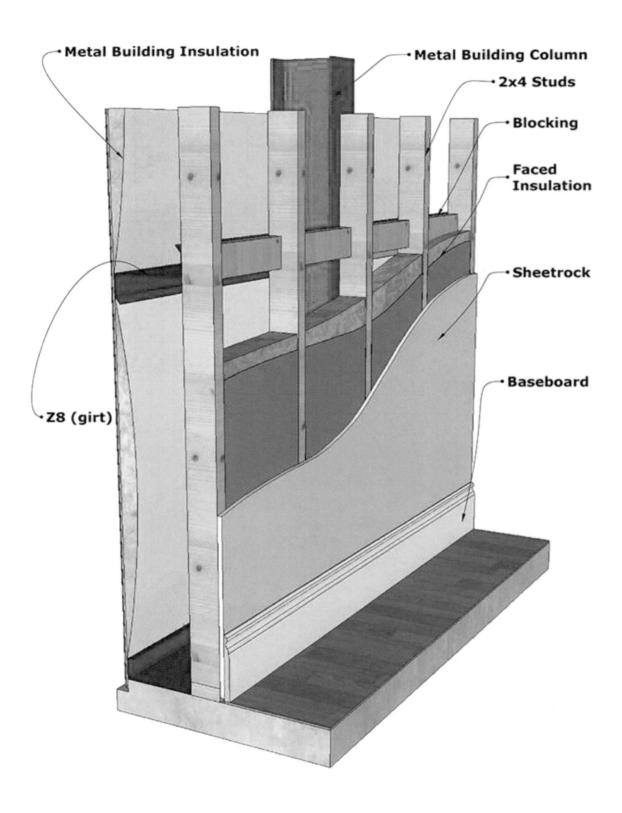

Metal Building Insulation

Metal Building Column

2x4 Studs

Blocking

Faced Insulation

Sheetrock

Baseboard

Z8 (girt)

Plan details

Square Footage Breakdown
Total Heated Area:4,590 sq. ft.
1st Floor:2,790 sq. ft.
2nd Floor:1,800 sq. ft.
Entry:233 sq. ft.
Porch, Combined:1,640 sq. ft.
Porch, Rear:620 sq. ft.
Porch, Front:620 sq. ft.
Loft:420 sq. ft.
Beds/Baths
Bedrooms:6
Full Bathrooms:4
Foundation Type
Standard Foundations: Slab
Exterior Walls
Standard Type(s):Metal
Optional Type(s):2x6
Dimensions
Width:113' 0"
Depth:60' 0"
Max Ridge Height:28' 6"
Garage
Type: Detached
Area:1090 sq. ft.
Count:2 cars
Entry Location: Side
Ceiling Heights
Floor / Height: First Floor / 9' 0"Second Floor / 8' 0"
Roof Details
Primary Pitch:12 on 5
Secondary Pitch:12 on 2
Framing Type: PEMB And Stick

Barndominium-Style House Plan with Cathedral Ceiling Garage

Experience the perfect blend of comfort and functionality with this exceptional 1-story barndominium-style house plan. Designed with 2x6 exterior walls, this home offers durability and insulation for optimal living conditions. With 3 bedrooms, 2.5 baths, and 2,191 square feet of heated living space, it provides ample room for everyday living.

The exterior of the house features a welcoming 10'-deep porch that wraps around three sides, offering a generous 1,360 square feet of covered outdoor space. This allows you to enjoy the outdoors and create a seamless connection between indoor and outdoor living.

As you enter the home, you'll be greeted by an open-concept front area with a cathedral ceiling, adding a sense of spaciousness and elegance. The great room, complete with a fireplace, offers stunning views across the porch, while the dining room provides direct access to the porch through sliding doors, making it convenient for outdoor dining and entertaining.

The master suite is a private retreat, featuring a large walk-in closet with direct access to the laundry room for added convenience. This thoughtful design element simplifies the task of managing your wardrobe and laundry.

Nearby, two additional bedrooms share a hall bath, providing flexibility to utilize these spaces as home offices or hobby areas based on your individual needs and preferences.

The garage is designed with practicality in mind, boasting a cathedral ceiling, drive-through capability, and ample shop space. This ensures that you have sufficient room for parking and storage, as well as a dedicated area for pursuing your hobbies or projects.

Embrace the comfort, functionality, and thoughtful design of this remarkable 1-story barndominium-style house plan. Its spacious layout, covered porch, and convenient features make it an ideal choice for those seeking a harmonious blend of indoor and outdoor living, all within a stylish and practical residence.

Floor Plan

Main Level

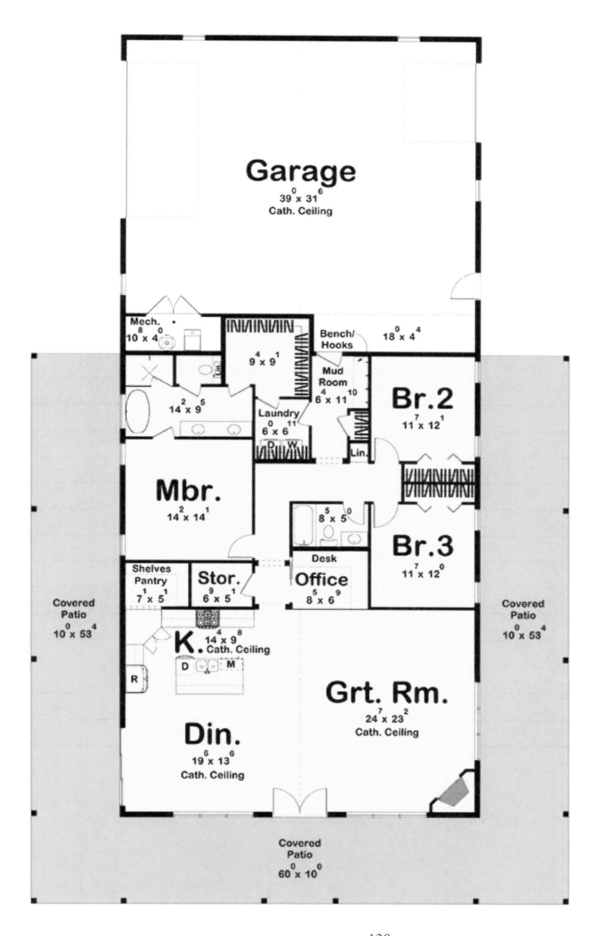

Garage
39⁰ x 31⁶
Cath. Ceiling

Mech.
10 x 4⁸ ⁰

Bench/
Hooks

18⁰ x 4⁴

9⁴ x 9¹

14² x 9⁵

Mud
Room
6⁴ x 11¹⁰

Br.2
11⁷ x 12¹

Laundry
6⁰ x 6¹¹

D W

Lin.

Mbr.
14² x 14¹

8⁵ x 5⁰

Br.3
11⁷ x 12⁰

Shelves
Pantry
7¹ x 5⁵

Stor.
6⁹ x 5¹

Desk

Office
8⁵ x 6⁹

Covered
Patio
10⁰ x 53⁴

Covered
Patio
10⁰ x 53⁴

K.
14⁴ x 9⁸
Cath. Ceiling

D   M

R

Din.
19⁶ x 13⁶
Cath. Ceiling

Grt. Rm.
24⁷ x 23²
Cath. Ceiling

Covered
Patio
60⁰ x 10⁰

139

Plan details

Square Footage Breakdown
Total Heated Area:2,191 sq. ft.
1st Floor:2,191 sq. ft.
Porch, Combined:1,360 sq. ft.
Beds/Baths
Bedrooms:3
Full Bathrooms:2
Foundation Type
Standard Foundations: Slab
Optional Foundations: Walkout, Crawl, Basement
Exterior Walls
Standard Type(s):2x6
Dimensions
Width:60' 0"
Depth:100' 0"
Max Ridge Height:27' 0"
Garage
Type: Attached
Area:1360 sq. ft.
Count:3 cars
Entry Location: Side
Ceiling Heights
Floor / Height: First Floor / 9' 0"
Roof Details
Primary Pitch:10 on 12
Secondary Pitch:3 on 12

One-Level Barndominium Style House Plan with 10' Deep Wraparound Porch

Step inside this inviting Barndominium-style house plan, where a spacious 10'-deep porch warmly welcomes you. This thoughtfully designed home offers a simple, one-level layout that caters to everyday living.

As you enter, you'll be greeted by a soaring cathedral ceiling that adds a sense of openness and grandeur to the living space. The kitchen features a centered island, providing three seats for quick and casual meals, making it a convenient gathering spot for family and friends.

The master bedroom is a tranquil retreat, complete with a walk-in closet and a bathroom that features a unique wet room design. The wet room combines the tub and shower, offering a modern and efficient use of space. Bedrooms 2 and 3 share a Jack-and-Jill bathroom, creating a functional and private space for family members or guests. Down the hall, you'll find the laundry room, adding convenience to your daily chores.

This house plan was specifically designed with a Pre-Engineered Metal Building (PEMB) in mind, which is the most commonly used structure for constructing a barndominium. PEMBs can be engineered, fabricated, and shipped to any location in the world, significantly reducing installation time compared to traditional framed homes. They also allow for quick and convenient interior build-outs, as they don't require extensive roof load support. With a PEMB, your project can progress rapidly, ensuring a dry environment and facilitating efficient interior customization.

To enhance durability and insulation, this metal house plan is available with 2x6 exterior framing. Simply select this option from the Options menu to optimize the structural integrity and energy efficiency of your home.

Embrace the charm, convenience, and efficiency of this exceptional Barndominium-style house plan. Its welcoming porch, open living space, and practical features make it an ideal choice for those seeking a comfortable and stylish residence that effortlessly blends with the ease of everyday living.

Floor Plan

Main Level

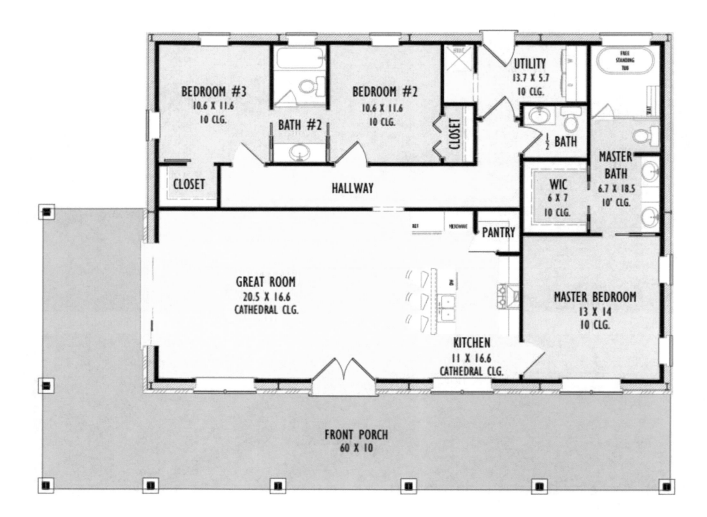

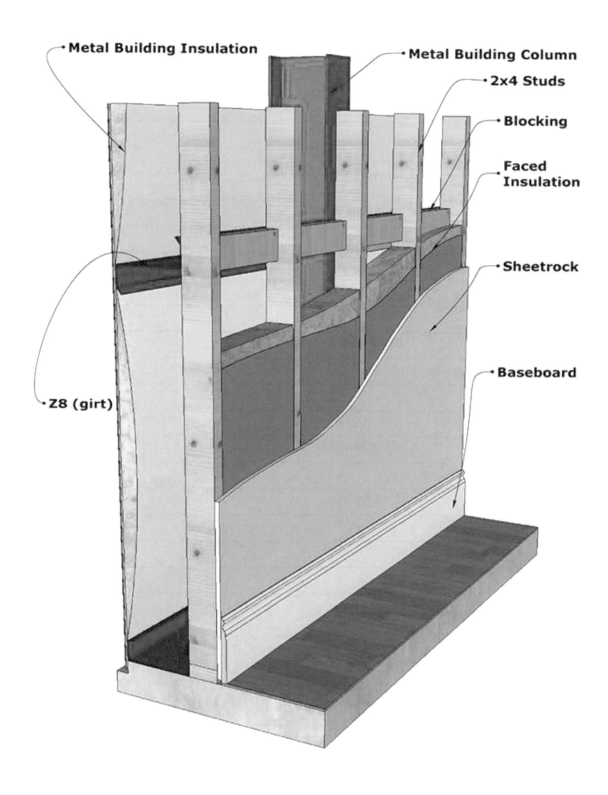

Metal Building Insulation

Metal Building Column

2x4 Studs

Blocking

Faced Insulation

Sheetrock

Baseboard

Z8 (girt)

Plan details

Square Footage Breakdown
Total Heated Area:1,750 sq. ft.
1st Floor:1,750 sq. ft.
Porch, Front:778 sq. ft.
Beds/Baths
Bedrooms:3
Full Bathrooms:2
Half Bathrooms:1
Foundation Type
Standard Foundations:Slab
Exterior Walls
Standard Type(s):Metal
Optional Type(s):2x6
Dimensions
Width:60' 0"
Depth:45' 0"
Max Ridge Height:19' 8"
Ceiling Heights
Floor / Height:First Floor / 10' 0"
Roof Details
Primary Pitch:5 on 12
Secondary Pitch:2 on 12
Framing Type:PEMB And Stick

2700 Sq Ft Barndominium-Style Home Plan with Wrap Around Porch and RV Garage

Welcome to this impressive barndominium-style house plan, spanning 2,700 square feet. The garage space alone encompasses 1,720 square feet, featuring one convenient drive-through bay and two RV-friendly bays. Additionally, a charming porch wraps around the front and left sides of the house, providing a generous 648 square feet of covered outdoor space for your enjoyment.

As you enter through the foyer, you'll notice a pair of doors on your right, leading to a home office with picturesque views to the front. On the left side, a captivating 2-story entertaining space awaits, complete with a cozy fireplace and a screened porch, adding to the charm and functionality of the home.

The island kitchen, accompanied by a walk-in pantry, is strategically positioned between the entertaining space and the dining room. The dining room features French door access to the porch, creating a seamless transition between indoor and outdoor dining, perfect for entertaining guests or simply enjoying a meal with family.

All three bedrooms are located upstairs, ensuring privacy and tranquility. The laundry room is also conveniently situated on this level, easily accessible from the hallway that overlooks the entertainment room below. This arrangement allows for efficient use of space and promotes seamless daily living. Additionally, the master bedroom features a spacious walk-in closet, providing ample storage for your belongings.

Experience the comfort and convenience of this well-designed barndominium-style house plan. With its expansive garage space, inviting outdoor areas, and thoughtfully laid-out interior, it offers a perfect balance of functionality and elegance for modern living.

Floor Plan

Main Level

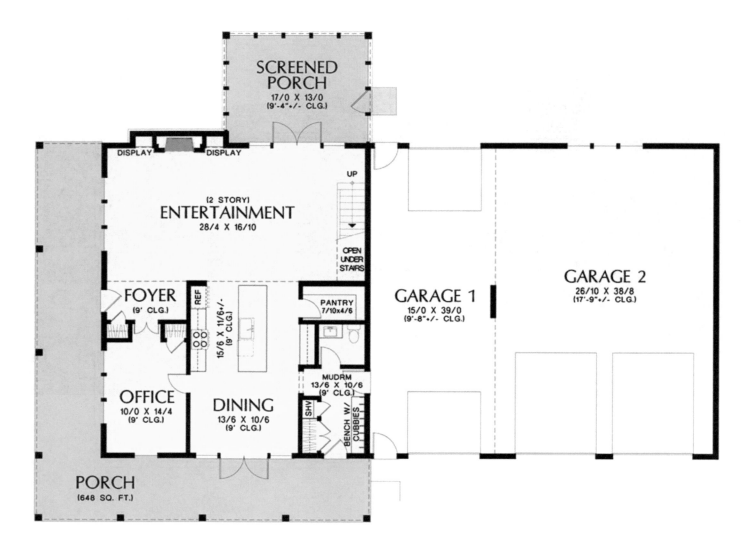

Plan details

Square Footage Breakdown
Total Heated Area:2,709 sq. ft.
1st Floor:1,371 sq. ft.
2nd Floor:1,338 sq. ft.
Beds/Baths
Bedrooms:3
Full Bathrooms:3
Half Bathrooms:1
Foundation Type
Standard Foundations: Slab, Crawl
Optional Foundations: Basement
Exterior Walls
Standard Type(s):2x6
Dimensions
Width:62' 0"
Depth:84' 0"
Max Ridge Height:28' 0"
Garage
Type: RV Garage, Attached
Area:1720 sq. ft.
Count:5 cars
Entry Location: Front
Roof Details
Primary Pitch:6 on 12
Framing Type: Truss

Barndominium Garage Apartment with Home Office and Game Room

Prepare to be impressed by this exceptional three-car garage plan, designed in a classic barn style. At first glance, the exterior showcases sliding barn doors that cleverly conceal a double car garage door measuring 18' wide and 11' tall. However, the true beauty of this design lies within.

Step inside, and you'll discover that the garage serves as the central hub of the layout, surrounded by inviting living spaces and separate offices. The main level of this classic barn-style garage features a wealth of amenities. On the left side, you'll find a full bathroom, a practical mud hall, and two bedrooms, with one of them perfectly suitable for use as a guest room.

Conveniently tucked under the stairs that lead to the second floor, you'll find a discreet area housing the washer and dryer. As you ascend to the second floor, you'll be greeted by a vaulted game room, providing a versatile space for entertainment and relaxation. Additionally, two storage lofts offer ample room for storing belongings and keeping the space organized.

The vaulted third floor of this remarkable plan presents a single bedroom apartment. The owners' suite occupies a generous portion of this floor, featuring a beautifully sized walk-in closet and a private bathroom. The bathroom boasts a shower room, complete with a free-standing tub, creating a luxurious and tranquil space. A great room, complete with a full kitchen, and convenient access to a covered deck, completes the functionality and charm of this barndominium garage apartment plan.

Experience the perfect blend of style, functionality, and comfort with this classic barn-style three-car garage plan. Its well-thought-out design, spacious living areas, and luxurious amenities provide an exceptional living experience for you and your guests.

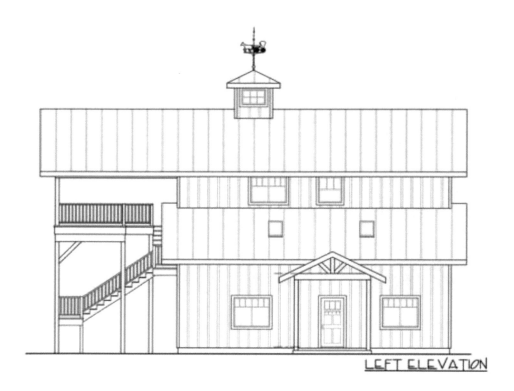

LEFT ELEVATION

REAR ELEVATION

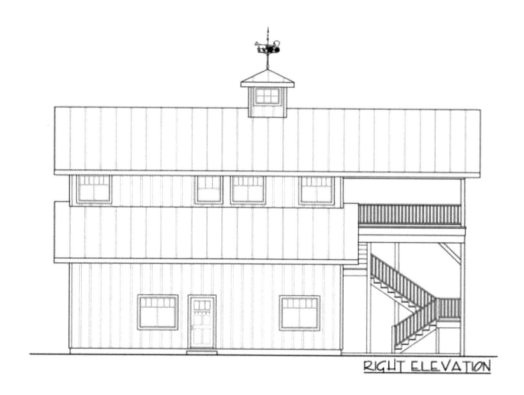

RIGHT ELEVATION

Floor Plan

Main Level

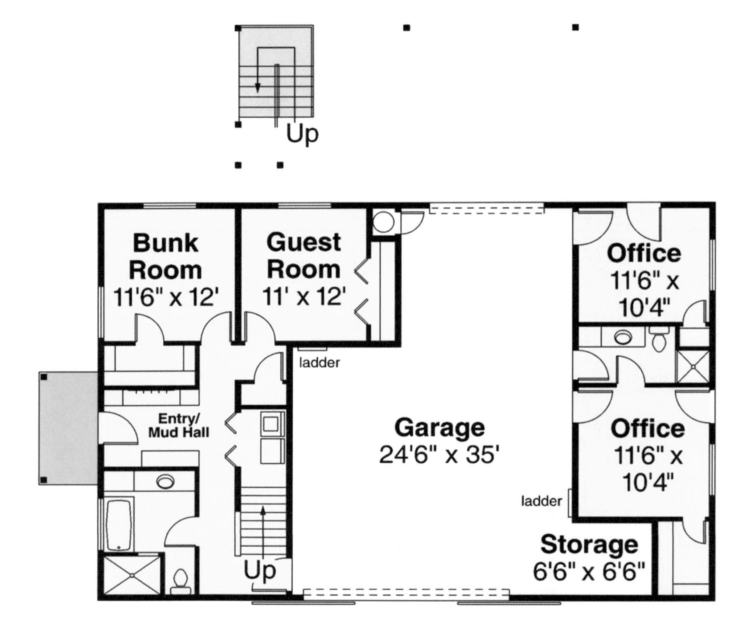

2nd Floor

Up

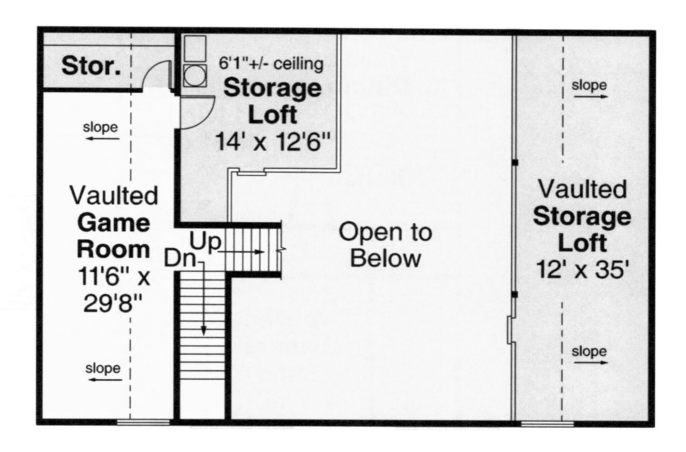

Stor.

slope

6'1"+/- ceiling
Storage Loft
14' x 12'6"

slope

Vaulted
Game Room
11'6" x 29'8"

Up

Dn

slope

Open to Below

Vaulted
Storage Loft
12' x 35'

slope

slope

159

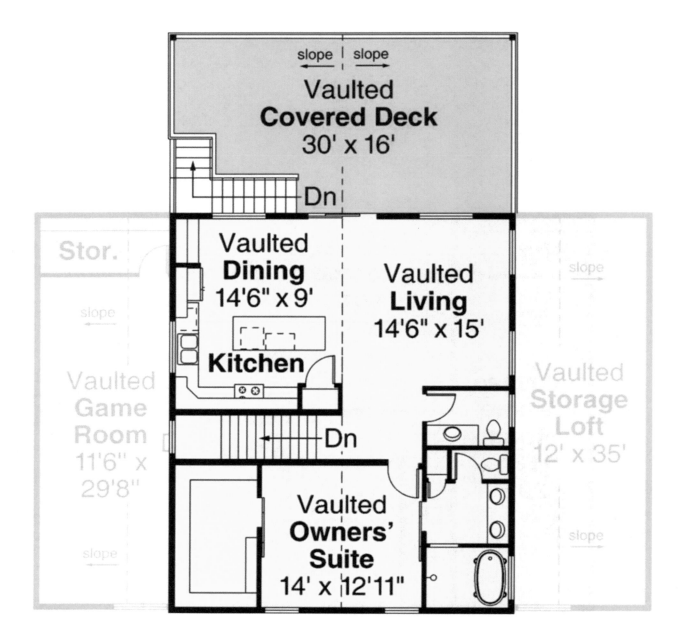

Plan details

Square Footage Breakdown
Total Heated Area:2,666 sq. ft.
1st Floor:1,136 sq. ft.
2nd Floor:468 sq. ft.
3rd Floor:1,062 sq. ft.
Storage:616 sq. ft.
Beds/Baths
Bedrooms:3
Full Bathrooms:3
Half Bathrooms:1
Foundation Type
Standard Foundations: Slab
Exterior Walls
Standard Type(s):2x6
Dimensions
Width:59' 0"
Depth:52' 0"
Max Ridge Height:38' 7"
Garage
Type: Attached
Area:808 sq. ft.
Count:3 cars
Entry Location: Front
Ceiling Heights
Floor / Height: First Floor / 8' 0"Second Floor / 8' 0"
Roof Details
Primary Pitch:6 on 12
Framing Type: Stick And Truss

2-Story Barndominium with Home Office and Wraparound Porch

Discover the cost-effective beauty of this two-story Barndominium with its rectangular footprint, keeping your budget in check without compromising style. Adding to its allure is a charming 10'-deep wraparound porch that enhances the curb appeal of the home.

Upon entering, you'll be greeted by tall ceilings that seamlessly unite the great room and dining area, creating a spacious and open atmosphere. The dining area flows effortlessly into the island kitchen, complete with a convenient walk-in pantry and a window above the double-bowl sink, allowing natural light to fill the space.

Adjacent to the foyer, you'll find a versatile home office, providing a dedicated space for work or study. Across from the office, the master bedroom awaits, offering privacy and tranquility. The master suite boasts two closets, providing ample storage for larger wardrobes. The ensuite bathroom is designed for comfort, featuring a luxurious freestanding tub and a dual-sink vanity.

On the upper level, a loft area overlooks the great room below and serves as a versatile space that can be tailored to your needs. From the loft, you can access bedrooms 2 and 3, which are separated by a compartmentalized bath, ensuring privacy and convenience for family members or guests. Dedicated storage space is also available, allowing you to easily organize holiday decorations and cherished memories.

The garage of this impressive Barndominium totals 2,304 square feet and features two 12' by 14' overhead doors and two man doors, providing ample space for parking and storage.

For the exterior, corrugated metal siding has been specified, adding a unique and modern touch to the home's finish.

Experience the perfect balance of affordability and style with this two-story Barndominium. Its practical layout, spacious rooms, and thoughtful design elements make it an exceptional choice for those seeking a cost-effective yet aesthetically pleasing living space.

Floor Plan

Main Level

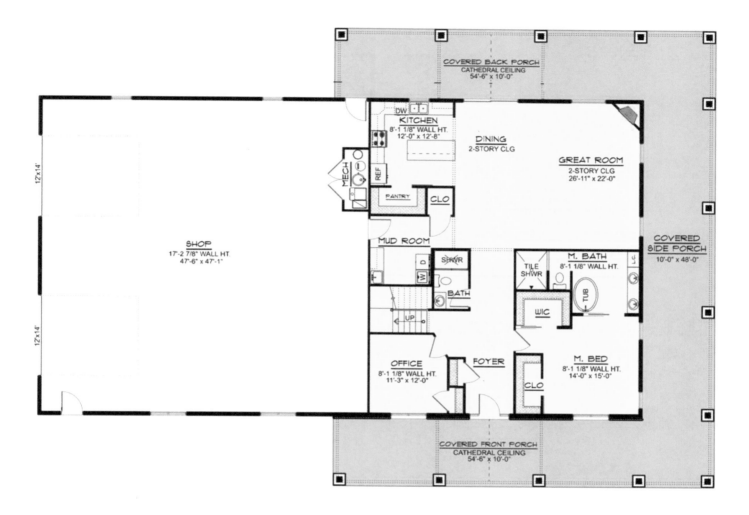

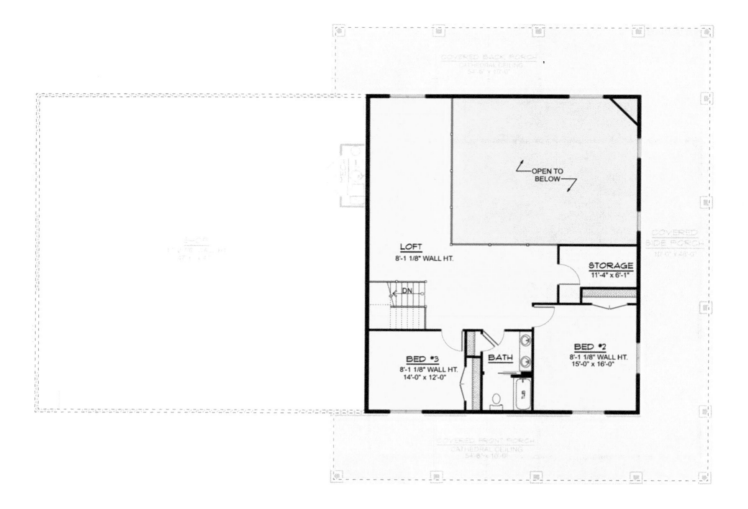

Plan details

Square Footage Breakdown
Total Heated Area:3,164 sq. ft.
1st Floor:1,920 sq. ft.
2nd Floor:1,244 sq. ft.
Porch, Combined:1,512 sq. ft.

Beds/Baths
Bedrooms:3 or 4
Full Bathrooms:3

Foundation Type
Standard Foundations: Slab
Optional Foundations: Walkout, Crawl, Basement

Exterior Walls
Standard Type(s):2x6

Dimensions
Width:88' 0"
Depth:48' 0"
Max Ridge Height:29' 9"

Garage
Type: RV Garage, Attached
Area:2304 sq. ft.
Count:2 cars
Entry Location: Side

Ceiling Heights
Floor / Height: First Floor / 8' 0"Second Floor / 8' 0"

Roof Details
Primary Pitch:6 on 12
Secondary Pitch:4 on 12
Framing Type:Truss

Made in United States
Troutdale, OR
11/05/2024

24260573R00095